Timeline of Ancient Rome

This timeline shows just some of the big events in more than a thousand years of Roman history.

Constantine the Great

Colosseum is built
The building of the Colosseum in Rome is completed.

Constantine becomes emperor
Constantine, the first Christian emperor, reunites the Empire under his rule.

80 CE — **98–117 CE** — **117–138 CE** — **284 CE** — **324 CE** — **476 CE**

Trajan is emperor
Rule of Trajan, whose conquests bring the Empire to its largest size.

Empire splits
The Empire is divided into an eastern and western half.

Last Roman emperor
Romulus Augustulus, the last western Roman emperor, is overthrown by Germanic tribes.

Hadrian is emperor
Rule of Hadrian, who builds defenses to protect the Empire.

Trajan's column in Rome is decorated with scenes from his wars.

Hadrian's Wall runs across Northern Britain.

Things to find out:

DKfindout!
Rome

Author and consultant: Peter Chrisp

Senior editor Marie Greenwood
Senior art editor Jim Green
Editor Olivia Stanford
US Editor Margaret Parrish
Design assistant Rhea Gaughan
Additional design Helen Garvey
Managing editor Laura Gilbert
Managing art editor Diane Peyton Jones
Pre-production producer Nikoleta Parasaki
Producer Srijana Gurung
Art director Martin Wilson
Publisher Sarah Larter
Publishing director Sophie Mitchell
Educational consultant Jacqueline Harris

First American Edition, 2016
Published in the United States by DK Publishing
345 Hudson Street, New York, New York 10014

Copyright © 2016 Dorling Kindersley Limited
DK, a Division of Penguin Random House LLC
16 17 18 19 20 10 9 8 7 6 5 4 3 2 1
001–291665–Sept/2016

A catalog record for this book
is available from the Library of Congress.
ISBN: 978-1-4654-5427-0

Printed and bound in China

A WORLD OF IDEAS:
SEE ALL THERE IS TO KNOW

www.dk.com

Contents

Temple

Citizen

Theatrical masks

BCE/CE
When you see the letters BCE, it stands for
"before common era," which are all the years
before 0. CE stands for "common era," which are
all the years after 0.

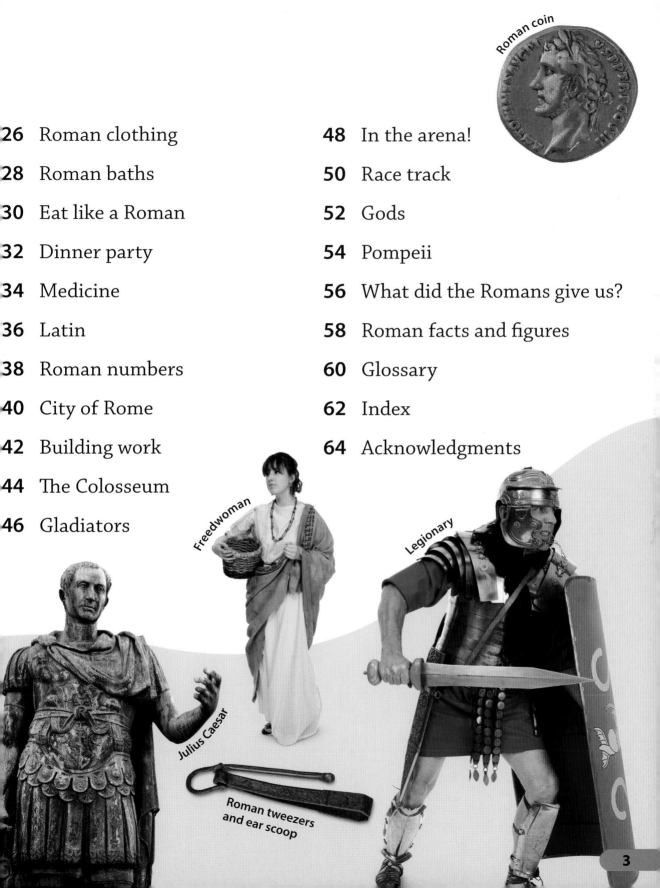

Roman coin

Freedwoman

Legionary

Julius Caesar

Roman tweezers and ear scoop

Who were the Romans?

Let's travel back in time, almost 2,000 years, to the Roman Empire. The year is 117CE, and the Empire is at its greatest size, ruled by Emperor Trajan. Let's talk to these two Romans, playwright Terentius and his wife, and ask them about their world.

Q: What is an empire and where is it?

A: An empire is a large area of land ruled by one person. The Roman Empire covers most of Europe and beyond.

Q: What is the capital city of the Empire?

A: The great city of Rome! It is built on the Tiber River in Italia. To us, it's the center of the world.

Q: Have you always had an emperor?

A: No. Until 27BCE, Rome was a republic, ruled by a government voted for by the people. Before that it was ruled by kings.

Q: How did you get to have such a big empire?

A: We conquered it with our armies. We are good at winning wars!

A: The first king of Rome was Romulus. It was said he built Rome after killing his twin brother, Remus, in an argument over where to put it. He then named the city after himself.

Q: Why are you called Romans?

A: Wherever we rule, people now dress like us, use the same coins, and some worship our gods. But we often add their gods to our own.

Q: Have you Romans changed the lands you conquered?

A: Today, it stretches 2,500 miles (4,000 km) east to west and 2,300 miles (3,700 km) north to south. About 60 million people live in it.

Q: How big is the Roman Empire?

Roman society

Within the Roman Empire, there were different groups of people, with different rights, or entitlements. Roman citizens had more rights than non-citizens, and slaves had no rights at all. However, slaves could earn their freedom and rise to a different level in society. The way people dressed helped show which group they belonged to.

Stola
This ankle-length dress, called a stola, was worn by married women.

White toga
The toga was a wool robe, draped around the body.

Tunic
This slave is wearing a simple tunic.

Palla
A palla (shawl) was worn over the stola.

Slave
Slaves were people who were owned by other Romans as property. They might be prisoners captured in war or the children of slave parents. As the Empire became bigger, so did the number of slaves.

Freedwoman
Through loyal service, slaves could earn their freedom. Former slaves were called freedmen and freedwomen. They kept close ties with their former owners, who might set them up in business, such as shopkeeping.

Citizen
The rights of a Roman citizen included being able to vote, to serve as a government official, and to wear a long wool robe called a toga.

Head wreath
Instead of a crown, emperors sometimes wore a wreath of laurel leaves. Sometimes the wreath was made from gold.

Purple toga
Emperors wore a purple and gold toga when they appeared in public.

Emperor
From 27BCE, Rome was ruled by an all-powerful emperor. He was high priest, lawmaker, and army commander-in-chief. After he died, he might even be worshiped as a god, as was the case with Emperor Augustus.

Toga colors
There were several types of toga. Each kind was worn at particular times or occasions, or by different classes of citizen.

Toga pura
This toga was made of plain wool. It was the everyday toga of ordinary citizens.

Toga picta
This purple and gold toga was worn by emperors.

Toga candida
A toga whitened with chalk was worn by men running for election.

Toga pulla
A dark brown toga was worn by men in mourning for a person who had died.

Toga praetexta
The toga praetexta was plain with a purple border. It was worn by high officials.

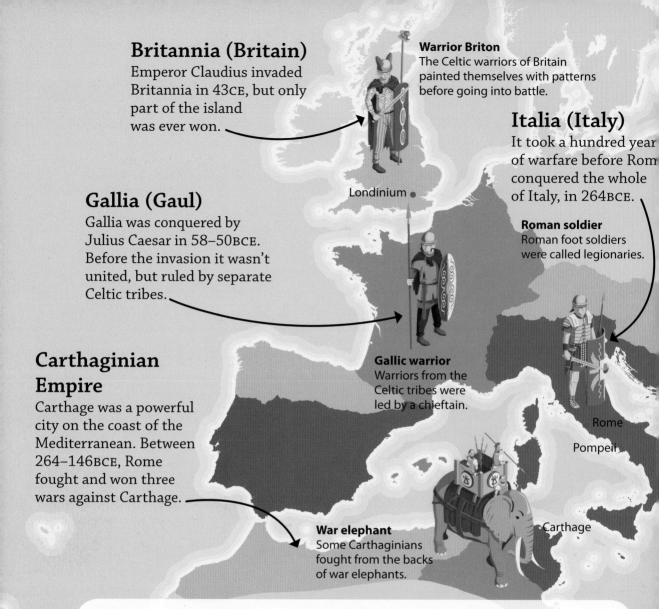

Britannia (Britain)
Emperor Claudius invaded Britannia in 43CE, but only part of the island was ever won.

Warrior Briton
The Celtic warriors of Britain painted themselves with patterns before going into battle.

Italia (Italy)
It took a hundred year of warfare before Rom conquered the whole of Italy, in 264BCE.

Gallia (Gaul)
Gallia was conquered by Julius Caesar in 58–50BCE. Before the invasion it wasn't united, but ruled by separate Celtic tribes.

Roman soldier
Roman foot soldiers were called legionaries.

Londinium

Carthaginian Empire
Carthage was a powerful city on the coast of the Mediterranean. Between 264–146BCE, Rome fought and won three wars against Carthage.

Gallic warrior
Warriors from the Celtic tribes were led by a chieftain.

Rome

Pompeii

War elephant
Some Carthaginians fought from the backs of war elephants.

Carthage

The Roman Empire

This map shows how the Roman Empire grew in size, through wars of conquest, between 146BCE and 117CE. It included all the lands around the Mediterranean Sea, which the Romans were able to call "mare nostrum," meaning "our sea." Before 27BCE, Rome was ruled by elected officials, but after it was controlled by emperors.

Constantinople
Athens
Mediterranean Sea
Alexandria

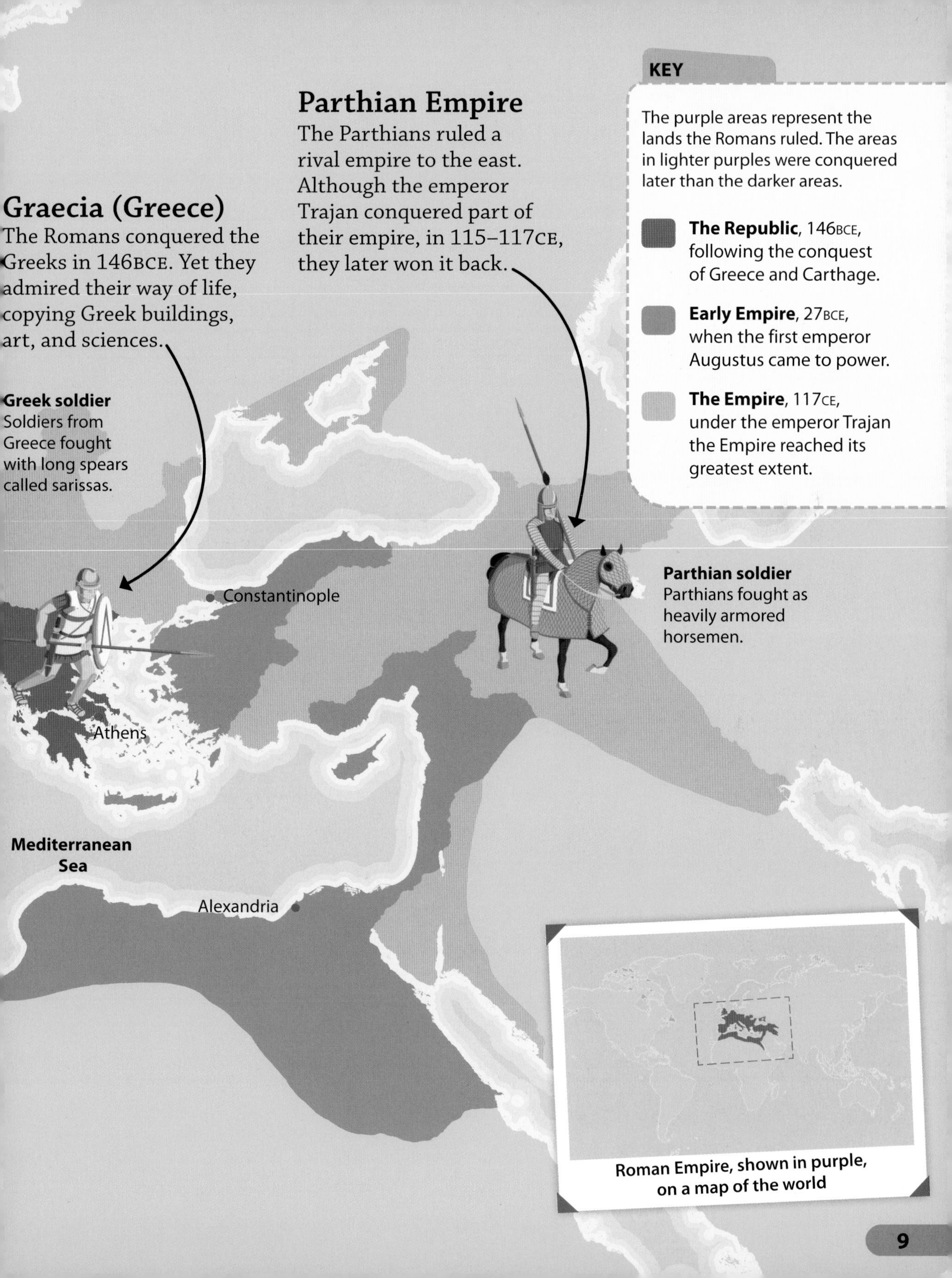

Graecia (Greece)

The Romans conquered the Greeks in 146BCE. Yet they admired their way of life, copying Greek buildings, art, and sciences.

Greek soldier
Soldiers from Greece fought with long spears called sarissas.

Parthian Empire

The Parthians ruled a rival empire to the east. Although the emperor Trajan conquered part of their empire, in 115–117CE, they later won it back.

Parthian soldier
Parthians fought as heavily armored horsemen.

KEY

The purple areas represent the lands the Romans ruled. The areas in lighter purples were conquered later than the darker areas.

- **The Republic**, 146BCE, following the conquest of Greece and Carthage.
- **Early Empire**, 27BCE, when the first emperor Augustus came to power.
- **The Empire**, 117CE, under the emperor Trajan the Empire reached its greatest extent.

Roman Empire, shown in purple, on a map of the world

Ruler of Rome

Julius Caesar was a great soldier and general. Before the emperors were in charge, the Senate, a group of noblemen, ruled Rome. In 44BCE Caesar defeated the Senate and made himself "Dictator." Here, we imagine how an interview with Julius Caesar might have gone.

FACT FILE

» **Name:** Julius Caesar

» **Dates:** 100BCE–44BCE

» **Location:** Rome

» **Fun fact:** He liked to wear a wreath to hide his bald head.

Caesar's head
Julius Caesar was the first living Roman to have his portrait on a coin.

Q: Caesar, which of your conquests are you most proud of?

A: It's very hard to choose between them. As I always say "veni, vidi, vici."

Q: "I came, I saw, I conquered"?

A: Exactly. You should really read the book I wrote about my success in Gaul. I also led two expeditions across the sea to Britain.

Q: Is it true that the Britons paint themselves blue?

A: Yes, when they go into battle. But we Romans will show them the proper way to live. We'll make sure that one day, they will even have bathhouses!

Q: Why did you go to war with the Senate, Caesar?

A: After successfully conquering Gaul (France) they ordered me to give up my army and return to Rome as a private citizen. I couldn't do that, could I?

Q: How did you defeat the Senate?

A: I am the best general Rome has. My loyal soldiers, toughened up by fighting those Gauls, are unbeatable. The Senate's leader Pompey was no match for me.

Q: People say that you've started acting like a king.

A: I am not a king, but the Empire needs a strong leader to keep it united.

Q: Why have you put your portraits on coins?

A: The people need to know who is in charge. Don't I deserve the honor, after all I've done for Rome?

Statue of Caesar
This is a bronze statue of Caesar dressed in military clothing.

I came, I saw, I conquered!

Q: Which are your greatest achievements?

A: I created a new calendar so a year now has 365 days. Before, there were only 355 and an extra month had to be added every few years. A month has been renamed "Julius" (July) in my honor.

Q: Aren't you worried about making enemies?

A: I'm good at winning over enemies. I forgave Brutus, who fought against me in the civil war. Now he's like a son to me!

Q: What are your plans for the future?

A: In three days, I set off east, to conquer the Parthians of Persia. Today I have a meeting with the senators at the Theater of Pompey. I'm just off to see dear Brutus there now.

Dagger

Stabbed

Caesar never got to fight the Parthians. In 44BCE, on the March 15, a day known as the "Ides of March," Caesar was killed. He was stabbed to death by a group of senators led by his former friend Brutus.

The emperors

A Roman emperor had enormous power. Some emperors used their powers wisely, while others were just not up to the job. Here are four of them. Were they good or bad leaders?

FACT FILE

» **Born:**
37CE

» **Ruled:**
54–68CE

» **Fun fact:** He raced a chariot in the 67CE Olympic Games.

Nero

Nero ruled well at first: encouraging art and culture, and boosting trade. But power went to his head. Nero murdered anyone who challenged him, including his own mother!

Good
- Gave many splendid public shows to entertain the people.
- Built theaters and set up athletic games and chariot races.

Bad
- Had anyone who did not agree with him put to death.
- Murdered his mother, wife, and step-brother.
- Was rumored to have started the Great Fire of Rome in 64CE.
- Blamed Christians for the Great Fire.
- After the Great Fire, he took over a large area of Rome to build a huge palace (the Golden House) just for himself!

FACT FILE

» **Born:**
63BCE

» **Ruled:**
27BCE–14CE

» **Fun fact:** He was just 18 when he became heir to dictator Julius Caesar.

Augustus

After defeating his rivals, Augustus made himself the first emperor in 27BCE. He had total power, but did not live like a king, claiming that he was just the "first citizen."

Good
- Brought peace and firm rule, after years of civil war.
- Lived simply, unlike a very rich and powerful ruler.
- Expanded the Empire.
- Built many fine public buildings and good roads.
- Funded the arts, such as literature.

Bad
- Took power by force, killing his rivals.

Verdict: Good

Verdict: Bad

Trajan

Trajan was a great general, whose success and popularity led to him being adopted by the emperor Neva. Trajan's conquests saw the Empire expand to its maximum size.

Good

- Expanded the Empire.

- Built a new forum in Rome, using money he won in war.

- Provided funding to help educate orphans and poor children in Rome.

- Reduced taxes.

Bad

- His expansion of the Empire made it so big that it became hard to rule well.

- Forced thousands of prisoners of war to fight as gladiators.

Verdict: Good

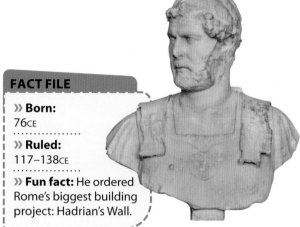

Hadrian

Hadrian, who followed Trajan, gave up some of the Empire's earlier conquests to strengthen the Empire's borders. He was possibly the hardest working emperor.

Good

- A very good administrator, he made the Empire more secure.

- Built strong frontier defenses, such as Hadrian's Wall, to stop northern tribes from attacking Britannia.

- Traveled widely around the Empire.

- A cultured man, he wrote poetry and designed buildings.

- Built many new public buildings and rebuilt others, including the Pantheon.

Bad

- His travels meant he was often away from Rome, making him unpopular there.

- Executed several senators who had plotted against him, and then denied it!

Verdict: Good

Roman army

The Roman army was made up of around 28 legions, each with about 5,000 soldiers, or legionaries, who fought on foot. They were helped by auxiliaries, who were fighters from lands conquered by the Romans. They brought extra skills that the legionaries may not have had, and included cavalrymen, archers, and slingers.

Slingers

Slinger auxiliaries could fire stones at the enemy with deadly accuracy. They came from islands southeast of Spain, where boys were trained to use a sling from a very early age.

Leather bag for carrying stones

Ways of fighting

Legionaries grouped themselves in various different ways when fighting, to give themselves the best possible protection and to help them attack the enemy more effectively.

Testudo
These soldiers are grouped into a testudo (Latin for "tortoise"). Holding shields over their heads gives the men a hard, protective "shell," just like a tortoise!

Bare shins
Only the lower legs, or shins, of the legionaries were left unprotected.

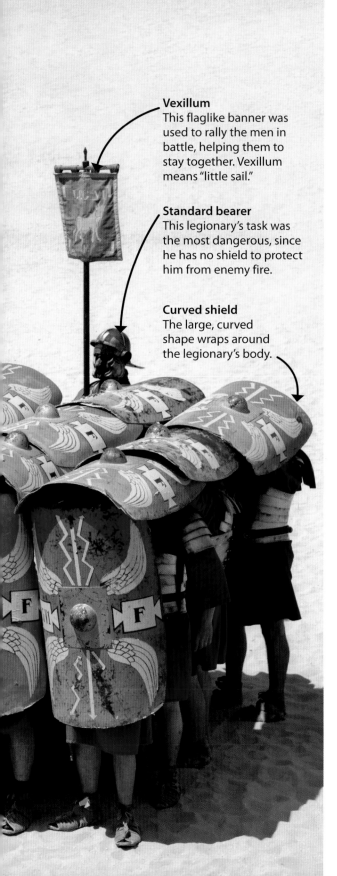

Vexillum
This flaglike banner was used to rally the men in battle, helping them to stay together. Vexillum means "little sail."

Standard bearer
This legionary's task was the most dangerous, since he has no shield to protect him from enemy fire.

Curved shield
The large, curved shape wraps around the legionary's body.

Army organization

Legions were broken up into smaller units, called cohorts and centuries. This made it easier to manage such a large group of men. Each cohort or century had its own leader.

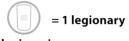 = 1 legionary

80 legionaries

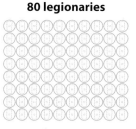

Century
A century consisted of 80 men. They were commanded by an army officer called a centurion.

 = 1 century

6 centuries

Cohort
A cohort was made up of six centuries grouped together, making 480 soldiers in all. They were led by a more senior centurion than the ones in charge of each century.

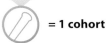 = 1 cohort

10 cohorts

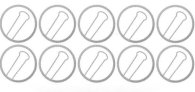

Legion
As well as 10 cohorts of foot soldiers, there were around 120 horsemen, who acted as messengers and scouts. The commander of a legion was appointed by the emperor, and was called a legatus.

 = 1 legion

Roman soldiers

Roman foot soldiers, called legionaries, had full-time jobs in the army. They were highly trained, well-armed, and always ready for battle. Lots of exercise, such as running and swimming, kept them fighting fit. This made the Roman army the most feared in the ancient world.

Legionary
Legionaries all wore the same clothing and had the same equipment. This helped them fight together as a group. They were led by a centurion.

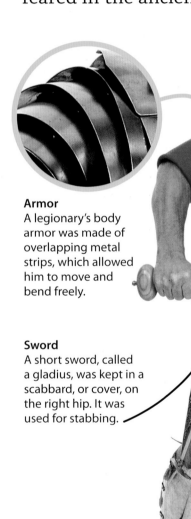

Helmet
A helmet, with cheek flaps to protect the face, covered most of the head, but let the soldier see and hear clearly.

Armor
A legionary's body armor was made of overlapping metal strips, which allowed him to move and bend freely.

Sword
A short sword, called a gladius, was kept in a scabbard, or cover, on the right hip. It was used for stabbing.

Shield
A long curved wooden shield, with a central bronze boss (plate), protected most of the legionary's body.

Sandals
Leather sandals had soles lined with iron studs, to stop them from wearing out on long marches.

Helmet crest
Centurions wore a sideways crest on their helmets, made from horsehair. This made them easy to see on the battlefield.

Centurion
A centurion was an officer in command of 80 legionaries. His helmet crest made him stand out from the other men, and he often carried a stick.

Stick
Centurions were strict. They carried a stick, using it to strike any legionary who was slow to obey orders.

Medals
These seven metal plates are medals, won by the centurion for bravery in battle.

Mail shirt
Centurions wore armor made of mail, which is hundreds of tiny iron rings linked together. They allowed for good protection against the thrust of a sword or dagger.

Greaves
The centurion's shins were protected with metal guards, called greaves.

A soldier's pack could weigh 90 lb (40 kg) and included food and tools.

At work

Although the Romans lived 2,000 years ago, many of the jobs they did are still done by people today. What job do you think you would have done if you lived in Roman times?

Baker

Romans usually bought their bread from a bakery. The loaves were baked in a round oven. Roman bakers were also millers. They ground grain into flour, using mills powered by donkeys or horses.

Actor

Romans loved the theater, especially since it was free! Actors performed on a semicircular stage. Some actors were big stars, with devoted fans, just like today. However, unlike modern actors, they usually wore masks. These showed what the character was feeling, for example, happiness, sadness, fear, or surprise.

Roman theater in Bosra, Syria

Engineer

Aqueduct in Segovia, Spain

Roman engineers, who designed buildings like this aqueduct, were highly skilled. Aqueducts were used to channel water to towns and cities. The aqueduct had to be built at exactly the right angle to ensure the water flowed smoothly.

Lawyer

Let justice be your cause!

Roman lawyers had to make long speeches, to persuade people to see their point of view. Lawyers either accused or defended people brought to trial for crimes, such as theft or murder. Many speeches by Roman lawyers can still be read today.

Teacher

Roman teachers ran schools, which were just for boys. Classes usually took place in the teacher's own home. Teachers used a tablet made of wax and a pointed stick, called a stylus, to teach children how to write.

Doctor

Roman doctors used instruments that are still in use today, such as sharp scalpels for cutting and forceps (tweezers) for removing splinters. The Romans believed that gods could help them get well, so doctors combined practical skills with religious rituals.

Surgeon's knife

Surgical forceps

Farmer

In Roman times, most people lived in the countryside and worked as farmers. Much of the hard work, such as raising animals and growing crops, was done by slaves.

Shopkeeper

Shops were found on the ground floor of houses and sold everything. Even takeout food was available! In 107–110CE, the emperor Trajan built a shopping center with more than 150 shops.

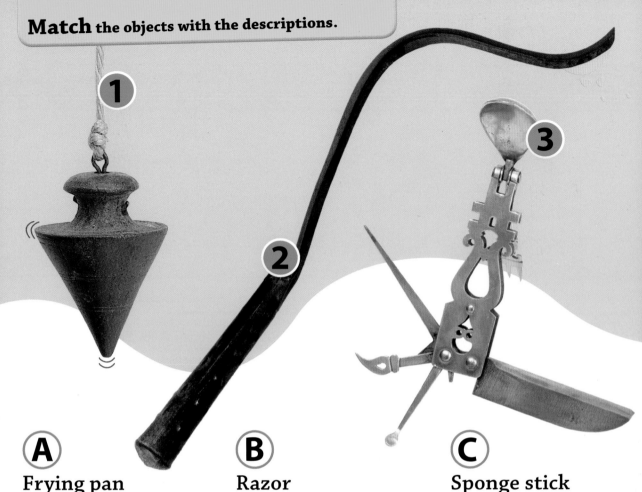

A

Frying pan

This Roman soldier's frying pan has a folding handle. This meant that it could be easily packed away into his baggage or stored for later use.

B

Razor

Roman barbers shaved their customers using a razor. This had to be regularly resharpened on a piece of leather called a strop.

C

Sponge stick

Toilet paper had not been invented in Roman times. Instead, people used a sea sponge on a long stick.

Everyday things

While life in Roman times was very different from how we live our lives today, some things were similar. Here's a collection of items that people used in Roman times. Some of them you may recognize, while others may seem strange. See if you can match each item with its description.

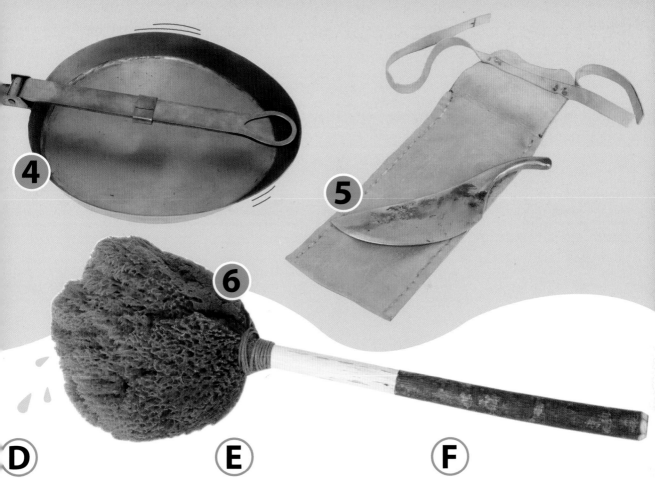

④

⑤

⑥

D

Plumb line

To determine if a wall or doorway was straight, Roman builders used a plumb line. This is a lead weight dangled on a length of string.

E

Folding tool

This folding device, like a pen knife, combines a spoon, knife, and other tools. It may have belonged to a traveler, such as a merchant.

F

Strigil

Instead of soap, Romans rubbed themselves with olive oil, and then scraped their skin clean with a curved metal tool, called a strigil.

Public toilet

Roman towns had public toilets, where people sat side by side! They were flushed by flowing water. Water also flowed through a channel on the floor and sponges were rinsed in this after use, and then left for the next visitor.

I'm not sure about her. She looks like the lazy type to me…

Buying a slave

You could buy a slave in the marketplace, just like you would buy any other goods you wanted. A buyer would look very carefully at the slaves on sale, checking for signs of carelessness, laziness, a bad temper, or poor health.

Slaves

Slaves were men, women, and children who were owned as property. If they disobeyed their owner, they might be harshly punished. Most Romans saw nothing wrong in owning slaves. However, many believed that they had a duty to treat their slaves well.

WOW!

! Some slaves wore **tags** saying who owned them, in case they **ran away**.

A runaway slave would be returned to the address on the tag.

Slaves served food and wine at mealtimes.

A trusted slave delivered letters and ran errands.

Slaves at work

Rich Romans had slaves to do almost everything for them. Slaves helped their master or mistress to dress in the morning and to get ready for bed at night. Slaves also prepared and served all their meals, cleaned up after them, and even entertained them.

A female slave would dress a Roman lady's hair.

Changing roles

A special holiday for slaves was held every year in late December. This was during the Saturnalia festival, which honored Saturn, the father of Jupiter. For one day, slaves swapped places with their owners, who served them.

Some owners treated their slaves to a special feast.

You have served me well. I therefore give you your freedom.

Wow! Now I am free!

Freeing a slave

Slaves who were loyal and worked hard could be rewarded by being given their freedom. Many slaves were highly skilled and, once they were free, went on to run successful businesses and even have their own slaves.

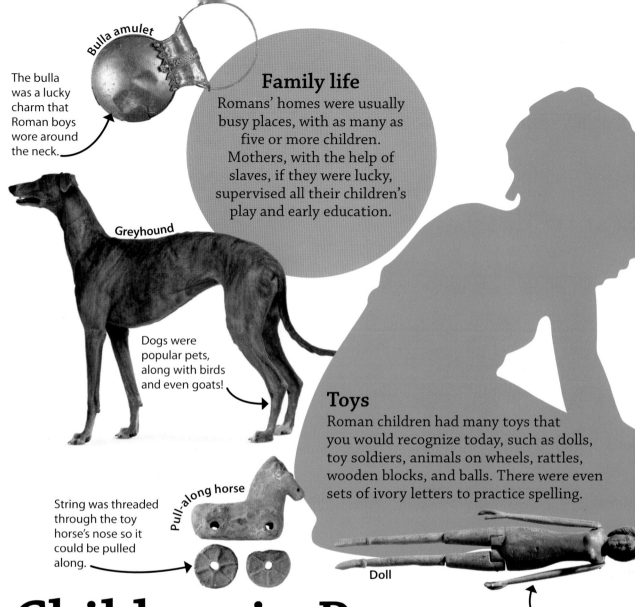

Bulla amulet

The bulla was a lucky charm that Roman boys wore around the neck.

Family life

Romans' homes were usually busy places, with as many as five or more children. Mothers, with the help of slaves, if they were lucky, supervised all their children's play and early education.

Greyhound

Dogs were popular pets, along with birds and even goats!

Toys

Roman children had many toys that you would recognize today, such as dolls, toy soldiers, animals on wheels, rattles, wooden blocks, and balls. There were even sets of ivory letters to practice spelling.

Pull-along horse

String was threaded through the toy horse's nose so it could be pulled along.

Doll

Children in Rome

Girls played with dolls, made from wood or bone. This one has moveable arms and legs.

Roman children were very much like children are today. At home, they had toys, played games, and kept pets. Some of them also went to school, although it was very rare for a girl to go. Many children, especially from rich families, were educated at home, taught by either their parents, slaves, or hired tutors.

Ink pot

Reed pen

This reed pen has a carved nib.

Wax tablet

Older children wrote with a reed pen, dipped in ink, on sheets of wood or papyrus, which is paper made from reeds.

Education

At seven, boys might go to school, or be given a private tutor. They studied literature, math, and public speaking. Girls usually stayed at home to learn how to run a household. Poor children often had to work, helping their parents.

Young children practiced writing by scratching letters on a wooden tablet coated in wax.

Children learned to count by moving balls along a frame called an abacus.

Abacus

The game of marbles was already popular in ancient Rome.

Marbles

Animal knucklebones were used to play catching games, like jacks.

Knucklebones

! WOW!

Cats were **not popular pets** with children in ancient Rome. They were seen as a **nuisance!**

Home schooling

Rich Romans usually hired tutors to teach their children at home. Here, two teenage boys are seen reading to their tutor. A third boy looks like he has just arrived, possibly a little late for class!

Carving showing a Roman class, from Germany

Roman clothing

The Romans did not wear close-fitting tailored clothes, such as jackets or pants. Clothes for men and women were made of large pieces of cloth, draped around the body or tied with belts. The basic item was the tunic, made from two rectangles of fabric with two holes for the arms. It was knee length for men and longer for women.

Necklace
Roman women loved jewelry of all kinds, often made of gold and precious gems.

Gold border

Purple and gold
Purple dye was expensive. Only rich Romans, like the imperial family, could wear it.

Palla
The palla was a type of shawl. It came in many colors.

Stola
A stola was a long dress worn over the tunic.

Women's clothing

On top of their tunic, women wore an ankle-length dress, called a stola. Over this a shawl, called a palla, could be added. The palla might rest on the shoulders or cover the head, like a veil.

! WOW!

Emperor Augustus, who felt the cold, wore **four tunics** at the same time!

Men's clothing

Male citizens had the right to wear a toga, a wool sheet draped around the body. This was so important to Romans that they called themselves "the race that wears the toga."

Short hair
Roman fashions in hair changed over time, just like today.

Beard
Beards were made fashionable by the emperor Hadrian.

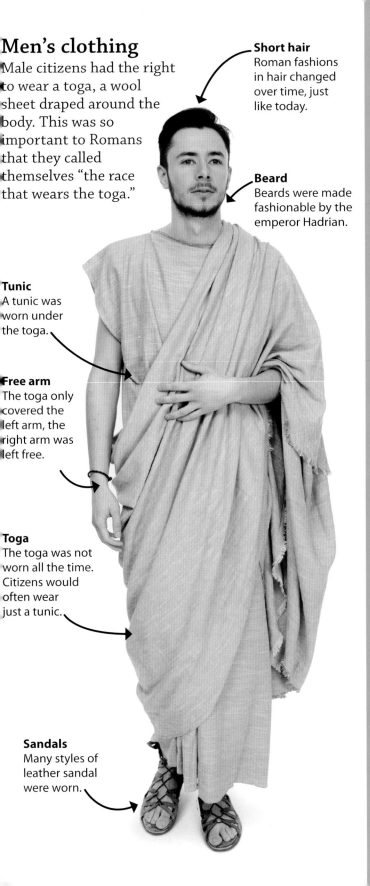

Tunic
A tunic was worn under the toga.

Free arm
The toga only covered the left arm, the right arm was left free.

Toga
The toga was not worn all the time. Citizens would often wear just a tunic.

Sandals
Many styles of leather sandal were worn.

Putting on a toga

Usually a slave would help a Roman put his toga on, since they were very long and heavy.

Step 1
The toga was a 18 ft (5.5 m) long semicircular wool sheet. Different colors of toga were used for different occasions. After you have put on your tunic, pick your toga.

Step 2
Drape one end of the toga over your arm and shoulder, making sure the fabric reaches the floor. Then wind the other end around your back.

Step 3
Pass the toga under your arm and back over the first shoulder again. Be careful not to let the fabric on your first arm slide off.

Step 4
Make sure the toga is secure. Now you're properly dressed and ready to go!

Roman baths

Every Roman town had a bathhouse for the local people. This was not just a place to wash, but also to exercise, relax, and meet friends. Men and women bathed separately. Big baths had separate areas for men and women. With smaller baths, men and women went at different times of day.

HOW TO USE THE BATHS

A **Apodyterium** Romans went to the changing rooms (apodyterium) first to undress. Slaves guarded any valuables.

B **Palaestra** Visitors might then go to the palaestra, an area for exercise. People used lead weights, wrestled, or played ball games to work up a sweat.

C **Natatio** They could then take a swim in the (unheated) swimming pool, called a natatio.

D **Tepidarium** In the warm room, slaves would rub visitors with scented oil and use a curved bronze tool called a strigil to scrape away dirt and dead skin.

E **Caldarium** Romans might visit the hot room (caldarium) next to sit in the steam bath. This was heated with hot air flowing under the floor.

F **Frigidarium** People visited the cold room (frigidarium) and jumped into a refreshing plunge bath to cool off.

Tepidarium
People often returned to the warm room at the end to relax and for a final rub with oil.

Furnace
The baths were heated by hot air from a furnace. Slaves brought a constant supply of wood to feed the fire. The hottest room was the one nearest the furnace.

Hypocaust
The floor rested on columns of brick, creating spaces for hot air from the furnace to pass through. This underfloor heating system is called a hypocaust.

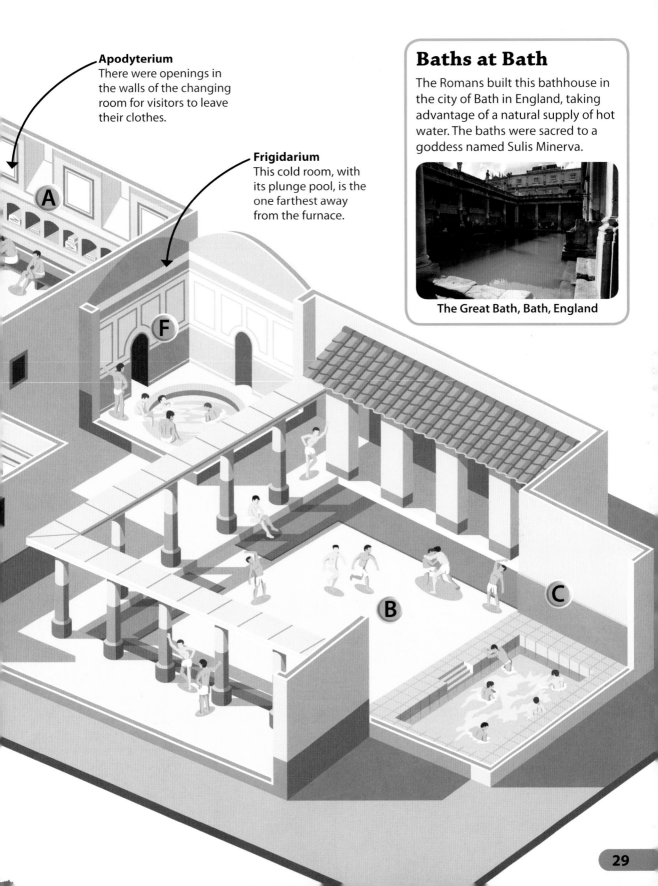

Apodyterium
There were openings in the walls of the changing room for visitors to leave their clothes.

A

Frigidarium
This cold room, with its plunge pool, is the one farthest away from the furnace.

F

Baths at Bath

The Romans built this bathhouse in the city of Bath in England, taking advantage of a natural supply of hot water. The baths were sacred to a goddess named Sulis Minerva.

The Great Bath, Bath, England

B

C

Eat like a Roman

Rich Romans loved to throw dinner parties, where they served course after course of unusual dishes. We can still read Roman cookbooks, which have recipes for flamingo tongues, ostrich brains, and boiled parrots!

Snails
Snails were such a popular food that they were raised on special snail farms, where they were fed on milk.

Garlic
The Romans liked garlic for its taste and because they thought it gave them strength. Roman soldiers ate garlic before going into battle.

Fruit
Romans enjoyed fresh fruit for dessert. They ate many types of fruit, including figs and pears.

Oysters

Oysters were eaten by rich and poor. Vast numbers of oyster shells have been found in Roman garbage dumps.

Fish

The Romans ate all kinds of fish. They also loved a spicy sauce, called garum, made from the rotting insides of mackerel and other fish.

I hear they eat flamingos ... I'm getting out of here!

Bread

Bread was the main food eaten every day by the poor. Loaves of Roman bread have been found in the ruins of Herculaneum, near Pompeii.

Dormice

Dormice were fattened up in special pottery jars before being eaten. A baked stuffed dormouse was a popular snack.

Olives

The Romans ate olives whole, but they also pressed them to make olive oil. This oil was used in cooking and burned in lamps.

Dinner party

This Roman painting shows the end of a dinner party. Dinner, or cena, often lasted for hours and included entertainment like music and dancing. Romans ate and drank while lying on couches while slaves served food and drink. The food here has been cleared away and the guests are now drinking wine.

WOW!

Romans ate with their **fingers**, but used a spoon for soup!

5

6

9

2

3

WHAT'S IN THE PICTURE?

1 Wall painting This painting is from a house in Pompeii.

2 Triclinium Roman dining rooms had three couches for guests to lie on. Only two can be seen here.

3 Table Food and drink was placed on low tables so it was in easy reach.

4 Bowl Diners washed their hands in bowls between each course.

5 Wreaths Rings of leaves were worn like party hats.

6 Pale skin This was fashionable for women and was a sign of high status (class).

7 Wine Romans added water to their wine to make it weaker.

8 Tableware Glass cups and bowls were expensive.

9 Couch Padded cushions made couches comfortable to recline on.

10 Loose, light clothes These were worn by the men, unlike the heavy toga worn in public. Their uncovered shoulders show they are relaxing.

33

Sage
This plant was sacred to the Romans. It was thought to have powerful healing properties.

Fenugreek seeds
Roman doctors prescribed seeds of the fenugreek plant for treating pneumonia.

Flax seeds
Crushed flax seeds were used to help heal wounds and soothe sore throats.

Black pepper
Medicines containing black pepper were used to treat many problems, including colds, earache, and toothache.

Chamomile
This plant was used to treat headaches, as well as liver and kidney problems.

Hook retractor
A hook was used to hold blood vessels out of the way during operations.

Ligula
This bronze instrument, a ligula, could be used to mix and apply ointments or remove earwax.

Medicine

Roman doctors used many medicines, made from lots of different plants, to fight disease. The Romans were also skilled surgeons, thanks to years of experience treating wounded soldiers and gladiators. In addition to using practical treatments, the sick prayed to the gods to help them get well.

Scalpel
Boils could be removed with a sharp scalpel.

Cucumber
The cooling effect of cucumber was used to fight fever and reduce hot and inflamed skin.

Spatula
Doctors used metal spatulas for mixing their own medicines and to apply them.

Ointment spoon
Metal spoons were used for applying ointment and giving liquid medicines.

Vinegar
Roman soldiers carried a vinegar drink called posca that was thought to be strengthening. Vinegar was also used to clean wounds.

Honey
The antiseptic, healing powers of honey were well known to the Romans, who applied it to cuts and wounds.

Fennel
Fennel had more than 20 medical uses, including treating eye problems and calming the nerves.

Greek doctors
The ancient Greeks were the first people to develop a scientific approach to medicine. Their theories and treatments were adopted by the Romans. In fact, most of the doctors in ancient Rome were Greek.

Latin

Would you like to speak some Latin, the language of the Romans? We've labeled this town street with Latin words, and how to say them. In fact, you might already use Latin without knowing it. Many European languages still use letters and words similar to ones in Latin. Thousands of English words come from Roman ones.

Panis
(PAN-iss
Bread

Thermopolium
(ther-mo-POLE-ee-um)
Snack bar

Tabula
(TAB-u-la)
Tablet

Puer
(POO-er)
Boy

Caput
(CAP-oot)
Head

Vir
(weer)
Man

Brachium
(BRAK-ee-um)
Arm

Crus
(croos)
Leg

Manus
(MAN-oos)
Hand

Via
(WEE-ah)
Street

Calx
(KAL-ix)
Heel

Genu
(GAY-noo)
Knee

Columna
(col-OOM-na)
Column

Ianua
(YAN-oo-ah)
Front door

Miles
(MEE-lays)
Soldier

Pisces
(PIE-sees)
Fish

Fenestra
(fen-ESS-tra)
Window

Puella
(POO-el-ah)
Girl

Corbis
(KOR-biss)
Basket

Mendicus
(MEN-di-koos)
Beggar

Domina
(DOM-ee-nah)
Woman

Maleus
(MAL-ee-oos)
Hammer

Canis
(CAN-iss)
Dog

Cave canem

A mosaic is a picture made up of tiny squares of stone or glass. This one shows a dog and the words "Cave canem." Can you guess what the Latin words mean? They say, "Beware of the dog."

Mosaic found in the city of Pompeii.

Roman numbers

The Romans used letters to stand for numbers, such as V for 5. We call these letters Roman numerals. Roman numerals were used throughout the Roman Empire for counting and pricing goods. Even after the end of the Empire, the numerals continued to be used throughout Europe for hundreds of years.

How numerals worked

The Romans only used seven letters to make all their numbers. Each has a set value, such as X for 10. Numbers without a matching letter are made by adding or subtracting the values of these seven letters. If a smaller numeral is to the right of a larger one, you add them, so LX stands for 60 (50 + 10). But if the smaller numeral is to the left of the bigger one, we take the smaller one away. So 40 is shown by XL (50 - 10).

! WOW!

The Romans had **no numeral** for **zero!**

1	2	3
4	5	6
7	8	9
10	20	30
40	50	60
70	80	90
100	500	1,000

Numerals now

Although Roman numerals are fairly complicated, we still use them for decoration. Look out for Roman numerals on clockfaces, coins, and on the dates at the end of television programs.

Alarm clock

Big numbers

To figure out a big number written in Roman numerals, first list the 1,000s, then the 100s, then the 10s, and last the 1s. Finally, add them together.

For example, **MMXVI** is

| **M** | **M** | **X** | **V** | **I** |

1,000 + 1,000 + 10 + 5 + 1

= 2,016

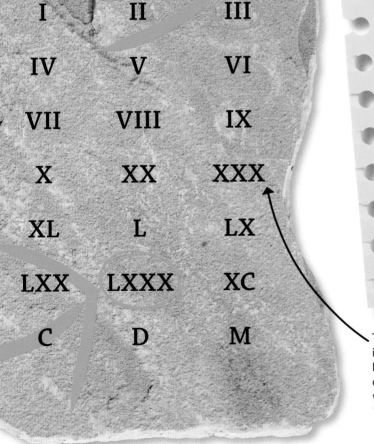

I	II	III
IV	V	VI
VII	VIII	IX
X	XX	XXX
XL	L	LX
LXX	LXXX	XC
C	D	M

Crack the code

Complete these addition problems on a piece of paper, then add up the answers to find out which year Pompeii was destroyed by the eruption of Mount Vesuvius. The answer is at the bottom of the page.

X + VII = ?

L - XX = ?

C ÷ V = ?

X + II = ?

Now add up your answers!

Today, we can turn a 3 into 30 by adding a zero. But the Romans couldn't do this. To write 30, they wrote the symbol for 10—X—three times.

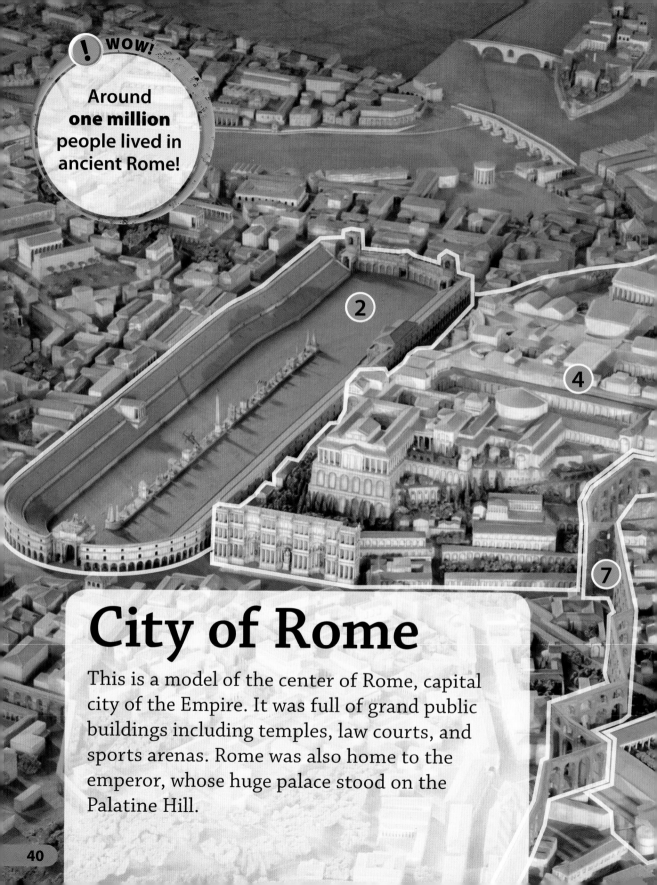

2

4

7

City of Rome

This is a model of the center of Rome, capital city of the Empire. It was full of grand public buildings including temples, law courts, and sports arenas. Rome was also home to the emperor, whose huge palace stood on the Palatine Hill.

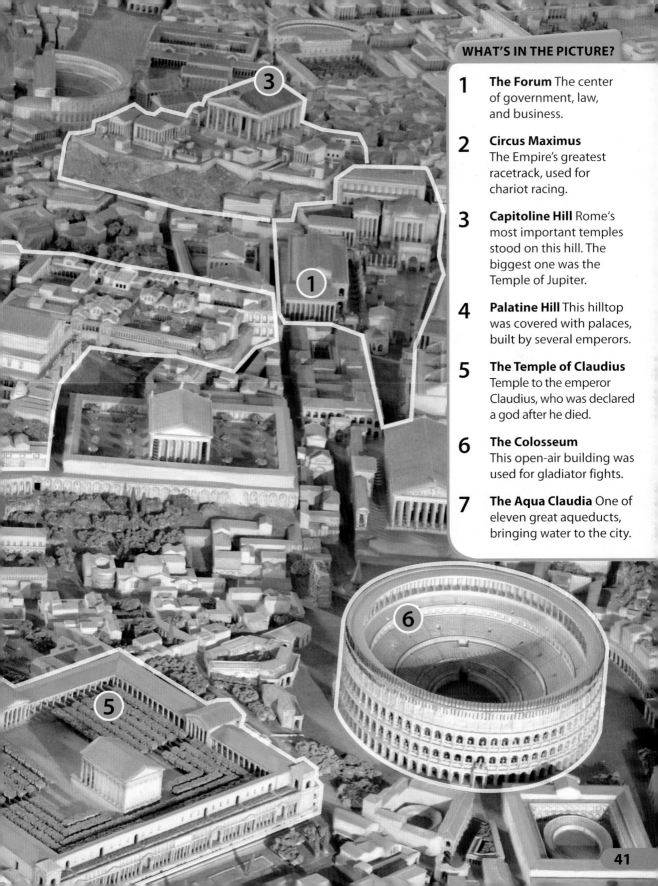

1 The Forum The center of government, law, and business.

2 Circus Maximus The Empire's greatest racetrack, used for chariot racing.

3 Capitoline Hill Rome's most important temples stood on this hill. The biggest one was the Temple of Jupiter.

4 Palatine Hill This hilltop was covered with palaces, built by several emperors.

5 The Temple of Claudius Temple to the emperor Claudius, who was declared a god after he died.

6 The Colosseum This open-air building was used for gladiator fights.

7 The Aqua Claudia One of eleven great aqueducts, bringing water to the city.

Building work

Roman builders copied the styles of Greek architecture, but built on a much grander scale. They made great use of arches, mass-produced bricks and concrete, and built the world's first domes. The Romans were so good at building that many of their aqueducts, temples, and bridges are still standing.

Arch

A building with arches is as strong as one with solid walls but is much quicker to build. The Romans used arches to build this aqueduct (bridge for carrying water) across a French river.

Pont du Gard, France

Insula

Town buildings were divided into blocks, called insulae (islands). The brick apartments of insulae could be up to seven stories high.

Insula in Herculaneum

Wall

A lot of building work was done by the Roman army. They built Hadrian's Wall to form a defensive barrier that separated the Romans in Britannia from the tribes farther north.

Hadrian's Wall, England

Insula in Ostia, Rome

Dome

The Romans invented the dome, a rounded roof used to span a wide space. This is the concrete dome of the Pantheon, a temple to all the gods built by Emperor Hadrian in Rome.

Temple of Bacchus, Lebanon

Temple

Roman temples look like Greek temples. But while the Greeks built using cut stone, the Romans used cheaper bricks. They saved stone for the facings (decorative features). Temples were used to honor gods, and some even honored emperors.

Pantheon, Rome

Column

In Rome, Emperor Trajan built a 125 ft (38 m) high marble column, decorated with scenes of his wars of conquest. His ashes were buried in the base.

Temple of Augustus, Croatia

Trajan's Column, Rome

Road

The Roman Army also built a network of long straight roads, with deep foundations. These were the best roads built until modern times. One of the most important roads they built was the Appian Way (Via Appia Antica).

Via Appia Antica, Rome

The Colosseum

The Colosseum in Rome was the Empire's biggest amphitheater, a building for open-air shows. It seated 50,000 visitors, who came to watch men, called gladiators, and wild animals fighting and being killed for entertainment.

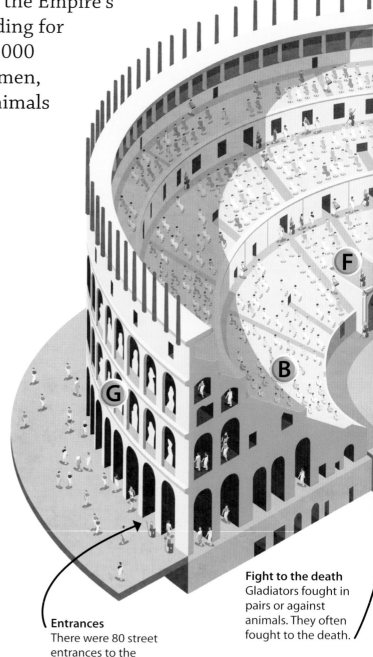

WHAT'S IN THE COLOSSEUM?

A   **Imperial box** The emperor and his family sat in a big box in the front row.

B   **Lowest level** The richest male citizens sat in the lowest level, where they had the best view.

C   **Middle level** Ordinary male citizens sat in the second level.

D   **Highest level** The highest level was for women and foreign visitors to Rome.

E   **Arena** The arena, or fighting area, had a wooden floor covered with sand to soak up blood.

F   **Gladiators' entrance** The show began with a parade by the gladiators, who entered through this gateway.

G   **Statues** The outer walls were decorated with statues of gods and emperors.

Entrances
There were 80 street entrances to the Colosseum so the audience could enter and exit quickly.

Fight to the death
Gladiators fought in pairs or against animals. They often fought to the death.

Women
Women were only allowed to sit in the top level seats. They were dressed more colorfully than the men, who wore plain togas.

Sunshade
These poles supported an awning, which could be extended to shelter the crowd from the hot sun.

Hidden rooms
Beneath the floor, there were tunnels with cages for wild animals, such as lions, rhinoceroses, and giraffes, as well as prisoners. They would be released into the arena through trapdoors.

Gladiators

Romans loved watching shows in which gladiators fought to the death. Most gladiators were slaves, convicted criminals, or prisoners of war, who were forced to fight. However, some free men, who liked fighting and sought the fame and wealth success brought, chose to be gladiators. There were several types, each armed in different ways.

PROVOCATOR

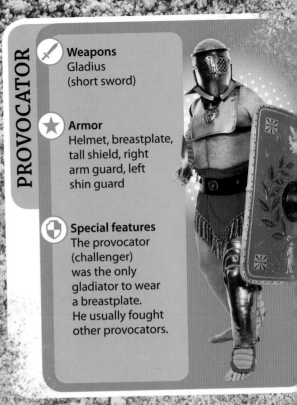

⚔ **Weapons**
Gladius (short sword)

⭐ **Armor**
Helmet, breastplate, tall shield, right arm guard, left shin guard

🛡 **Special features**
The provocator (challenger) was the only gladiator to wear a breastplate. He usually fought other provocators.

MURMILLO

⚔ **Weapons**
Gladius (short sword)

⭐ **Armor**
Big helmet, tall shield, right arm guard, left shin guard

🛡 **Special features**
The murmillo (fish man) had a tall helmet, often decorated with a fish crest. He was a slow, heavily armored fighter.

RETIARIUS

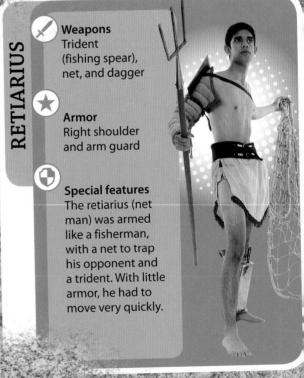

⚔ **Weapons**
Trident (fishing spear), net, and dagger

⭐ **Armor**
Right shoulder and arm guard

🛡 **Special features**
The retiarius (net man) was armed like a fisherman, with a net to trap his opponent and a trident. With little armor, he had to move very quickly.

SECUTOR

 Weapons
Gladius
(short sword)

 Armor
Rounded helmet,
tall shield, right
arm guard, left
shin guard

 Special features
The secutor
(pursuer) always
fought against a
retiarius. His helmet
was rounded,
making it harder
to get caught in
the retiarius's net.

THRAEX

 Weapons
Curved sword

Armor
Helmet, small
shield, thigh-length
leg guards

Special features
The equipment
of the Thraex
(also known as
a Thracian), was
based on that used
by the Thracians,
who were
long-standing
enemies of Rome.

HOPLOMACHUS

 Weapons
Gladius (short
sword) and spear

 Armor
Feather-topped
helmet, round
shield, right arm
guard, thigh-length
leg guards

Special features
The hoplomachus
("armed fighter"
in Greek) had the
round shield and
spear of a Greek
foot soldier.

In the arena!

It's the day of the games, and Memnon, the murmillo, is due to fight Felix, the retiarius. Memnon has never yet lost a fight, but he's getting older and slower. Felix has less experience, but he's young and fit. Who will win today?

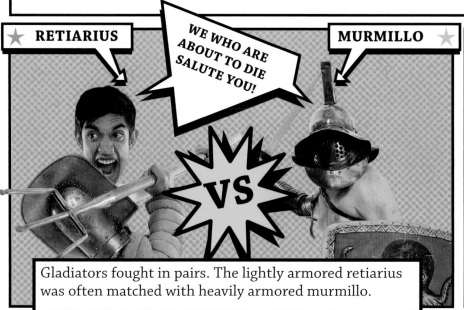

★ **RETIARIUS** ★

WE WHO ARE ABOUT TO DIE SALUTE YOU!

MURMILLO ★

Gladiators fought in pairs. The lightly armored retiarius was often matched with heavily armored murmillo.

The summa rudis (referee) raises his staff and orders the fight to begin.

OOOF!

Felix rushes forward with his long trident, hoping to take Memnon by surprise. His trident bounces off Memnon's shield.

Memnon now attacks back. He strikes at Felix, but catches his shoulder guard. The summa rudis watches on.

POW!

With his left hand, Felix now hurls his net, trying to catch Memnon's helmet. He misses, but tangles Memnon's short sword. Felix strikes again with his trident, but it bounces off Memnon's shield.

IF I CAN CATCH HIM IN MY NET, I WILL WIN!

SPLAT

OUCH!

Memnon gets tangled in the net and falls flat on his back. He raises his finger to show he surrenders and the fight stops.

There are shouts of "Spare him!" or "Kill him!" from the crowd. The final decision is the emperor's and he shows his decision with his hand.

KILL HIM!

SPARE HIM?

Victory!

RETIARII ARE THE BEST GLADIATORS.

Felix has won the fight, and shouts in triumph. If he wins enough, he hopes to be able to buy his freedom with his prize money.

Race track

Welcome to Rome's main chariot-race track: the Circus Maximus! Chariot racing was an exciting and dangerous sport. A chariot was a horse-drawn cart whose driver was called a charioteer. Charioteers were grouped into four teams: the Reds, Whites, Blues, and Greens. Each team had loyal fans, who cheered as the chariots hurtled around the track.

Spectators
There was seating for 250,000 people, five times more than the Colosseum could hold. Men and women sat together.

A

Biggest circus!
Circus Maximus is Latin for "biggest circus." It was 2,037 ft (621 m) long and 387 ft (118 m) wide.

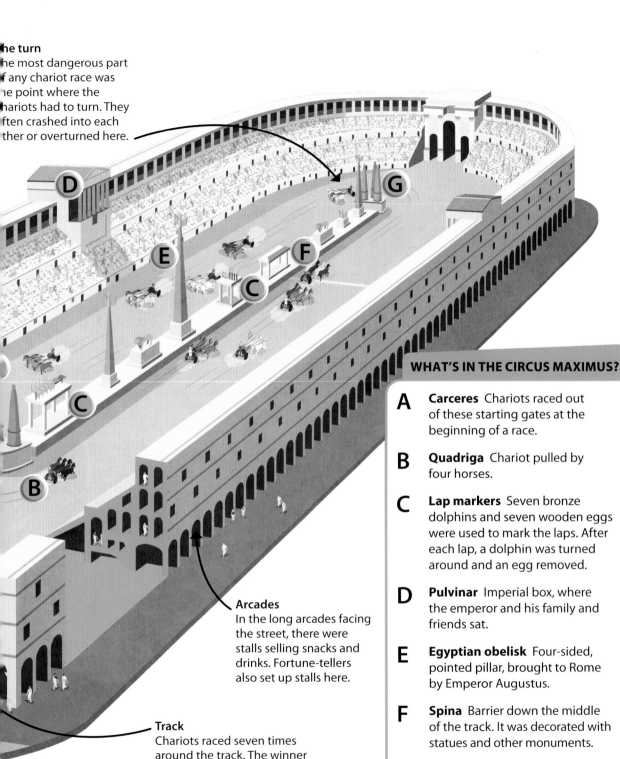

The turn
The most dangerous part of any chariot race was the point where the chariots had to turn. They often crashed into each other or overturned here.

Arcades
In the long arcades facing the street, there were stalls selling snacks and drinks. Fortune-tellers also set up stalls here.

Track
Chariots raced seven times around the track. The winner was the first chariot to complete all seven laps.

WHAT'S IN THE CIRCUS MAXIMUS?

A **Carceres** Chariots raced out of these starting gates at the beginning of a race.

B **Quadriga** Chariot pulled by four horses.

C **Lap markers** Seven bronze dolphins and seven wooden eggs were used to mark the laps. After each lap, a dolphin was turned around and an egg removed.

D **Pulvinar** Imperial box, where the emperor and his family and friends sat.

E **Egyptian obelisk** Four-sided, pointed pillar, brought to Rome by Emperor Augustus.

F **Spina** Barrier down the middle of the track. It was decorated with statues and other monuments.

G **Metae** Three tall posts at either end of the spina marked the turning point for the chariots.

Answer our quiz to find out which Roman god or goddess you are.

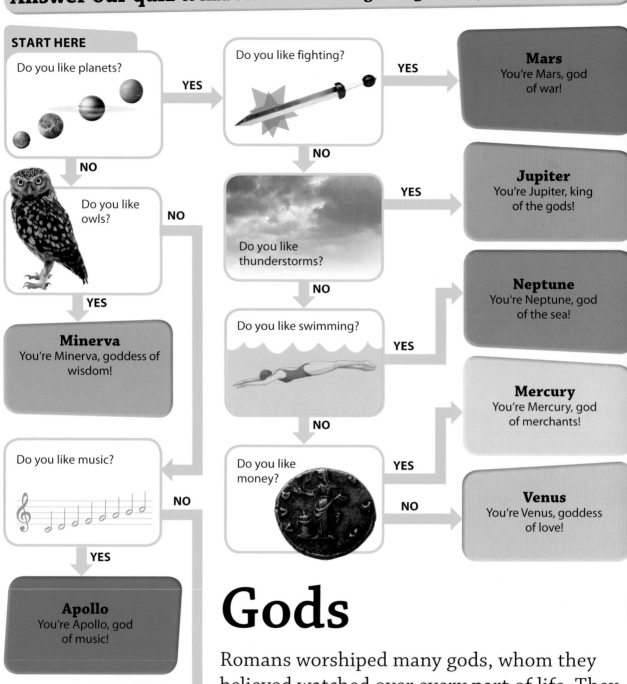

START HERE

Do you like planets?

— **YES** → Do you like fighting?
  — **YES** → **Mars** You're Mars, god of war!
  — **NO** → Do you like thunderstorms?
    — **YES** → **Jupiter** You're Jupiter, king of the gods!
    — **NO** → Do you like swimming?
      — **YES** → **Neptune** You're Neptune, god of the sea!
      — **NO** → Do you like money?
        — **YES** → **Mercury** You're Mercury, god of merchants!
        — **NO** → **Venus** You're Venus, goddess of love!

— **NO** → Do you like owls?
  — **YES** → **Minerva** You're Minerva, goddess of wisdom!
  — **NO** → Do you like music?
    — **YES** → **Apollo** You're Apollo, god of music!
    — **NO** → **Juno** You're Juno, queen of the gods!

Gods

Romans worshiped many gods, whom they believed watched over every part of life. They ranged from great ones, whom they built great temples for, down to household gods, who guarded the home.

Mercury

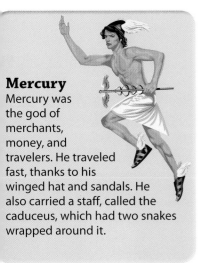

Mercury was the god of merchants, money, and travelers. He traveled fast, thanks to his winged hat and sandals. He also carried a staff, called the caduceus, which had two snakes wrapped around it.

Jupiter

Jupiter was king of the gods and special protector of the Roman Empire. He was god of the sky and storms, and was armed with thunderbolts. The eagle was his sacred bird.

Juno

Jupiter's wife, Juno, was the goddess of marriage and childbirth. Her sacred bird was the peacock. The Roman month of Junius (June), was named after her, and was thought to be a lucky time to marry.

Minerva

Minerva was the goddess of crafts and wisdom. She was born from Jupiter's head complete with her armor and weapons. Her sacred bird was the wise owl.

Mars

Mars was the god of war and also of farming. After Jupiter, he was the most important Roman god. The Roman month Martius (March) is named after him.

Neptune

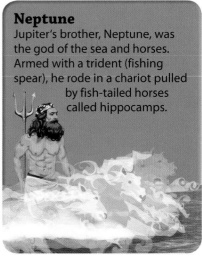

Jupiter's brother, Neptune, was the god of the sea and horses. Armed with a trident (fishing spear), he rode in a chariot pulled by fish-tailed horses called hippocamps.

WOW!

There was a goddess, named **Cardea**, who looked after **door hinges!**

Apollo

Apollo was the god of light, healing, music, and prophecy (telling the future). He played a musical instrument called a lyre, which Mercury invented.

Venus

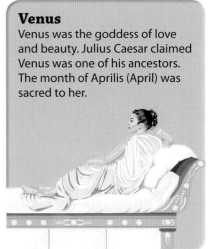

Venus was the goddess of love and beauty. Julius Caesar claimed Venus was one of his ancestors. The month of Aprilis (April) was sacred to her.

Pompeii

Mount Vesuvius today

On August 24, 79CE, Mount Vesuvius, a volcano in southern Italy, blew up, completely burying the nearby town of Pompeii. Although it was a terrible disaster, the town was perfectly preserved by being buried. This means that we can now explore the streets, houses, and shops of a Roman town.

The Forum of Pompeii

Victims of Pompeii

In addition to buildings, some of the victims who died at Pompeii almost 2,000 years ago were discovered. Their bodies were buried in ash from the eruption, which turned to rock around them. After they had rotted away, plaster was poured into the spaces they left to create casts.

Dog with collar

Dog
This is the cast of a guard dog. You can see the outline of its collar, which was made from bronze.

Column of the temple

The Temple of Jupiter

Plinian eruption

A volcanic eruption with a high cloud of ash and gas is called "Plinian" after the Roman writer Pliny, who wrote an eyewitness account of the disaster.

Mosaic of Egyptian animals

Round loaf

Mosaic
The houses of Pompeii were richly decorated with wall paintings and mosaics. This mosaic shows a hippopotamus and a crocodile.

Bread
This loaf of bread was found in a baker's oven in Herculaneum, Pompeii's neighboring town. It was preserved by boiling mud.

What did the Romans give us?

The Roman Empire fell in the fifth century CE, following invasions by foreign enemies. But even today, 1,500 years later, Rome still has an influence. We still travel along the routes of Roman roads, and coins and many buildings are based on Roman ones.

Lost and found

Concrete, now used everywhere in building, was invented by the Romans. Roman concrete was better than any made today, but the recipe got lost!

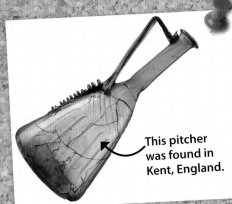

Glass

The Romans were expert glassmakers. They used it to make drinking vessels, vases, and pitcher. They were also the first people to use glass in windows.

This pitcher was found in Kent, England.

! **WOW!**

The Romans even invented books with pages!

Bridges

The Romans built some of the first permanent bridges. They were made from stone, brick, and concrete, and used single or multiple arches.

This Roman bridge across the Ouveze River in France is still in use today, despite being 2,000 years old.

Roman writers

Although the Roman Empire ended many years ago, we can still read the writings of Roman poets like Virgil. Virgil was seen by the Romans as their greatest poet.

This mosaic shows Virgil writing the *Aeneid*, his most famous poem.

12

Twelve-month calendar

Our 12-month calendar is Roman. Most of our months are named after Roman numbers and gods, such as March, named after the god Mars. However, July and August are named after Julius Caesar and Emperor Augustus.

Alphabet

Our alphabet is mostly a Roman invention. However, the Romans had 23 letters while we now have 26, and they only used capital letters. They would have written Julius as IVLIVS.

Roman alphabet

ABCDEF
GHIKLM
NOPQR
STVXYZ

Can you see which 3 letters are missing?

Answer: J, U, W

Cities

Across Europe, we live in cities founded by the Romans. In addition to Rome in Italy (above), Roman cities include London and York in the UK, Paris and Lyons in France, Cordoba and Seville in Spain, and Cologne in Germany.

Roman facts and figures

The Romans were a fascinating group of people. Here are some amazing facts you might not know about them!

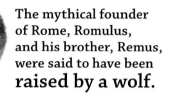

The mythical founder of Rome, Romulus, and his brother, Remus, were said to have been **raised by a wolf.**

HAIRY TRUTH!

There were people in Rome who earned their living by plucking other people's hair out, including their armpit hair!

52BCE Vercingetorix, a chieftain from Gaul (France), fought a war against Julius Caesar, but lost. He was led in chains through Rome in Julius Caesar's victory procession.

Constantine
was the first Christian emperor: he didn't worship the Roman gods.

50 🌍 250,000

Around 50 of today's countries were part of the Roman Empire.

The Romans built 250,000 miles (400,000 km) of roads.

ROME WAS RULED BY EMPERORS FOR OVER

400 YEARS.

ROMAN SOLDIERS had to serve for **25 years** in the army. They could walk up to **20 miles (30 km) a day** wearing heavy armor.

Romans made purple dye for clothes from SEA SNAIL SHELLS.

Romans used a two-handed jar called an **AMPHORA** to store all sorts of goods, such as olive oil, wine, and even garum (fish sauce).

7 Rome was ruled by seven kings before it became a republic.

73
Hadrian's Wall was 73 miles (117 km) long.

100
The opening games for the Colosseum lasted for more than 100 days.

Glossary

Here are the meanings of some words that are useful for you to know when learning about ancient Rome.

abacus Device with moveable beads, used by the Romans to count

amphitheater Big, oval, open-air building used for public shows, especially gladiator fights

amphora Two-handled jar, used by the Romans to store food, drinks, and oil

aqueduct Artificial channel used to carry water to a town

auxillary Member of the Roman army who was not a Roman citizen

bulla Amulet worn by Roman boys that was thought to protect them

centurion Roman soldier in charge of 80 legionaries

chariot Two-wheeled vehicle pulled by horses, used by the Romans for racing

circus Roman racetrack, for chariot racing

citizen Member of a state, with more rights than a non-citizen

civil war War fought between people who belong to the same country.

dictator Ruler with total power. Under the republic, dictators were appointed in times of emergency. But Julius Caesar made himself dictator for life

dome Large, rounded roof or ceiling with a circular base

emperor Ruler of an empire

empire Large area with different peoples, ruled by a single government or person

forum Central marketplace and public meeting area in every Roman town

freedmen and freedwomen Former slaves who bought or were given their freedom

garum Rotten fish sauce, eaten by the Romans

gladiator Type of fighter who entertained people by fighting in an amphitheater. Gladiators were usually slaves

Roman aqueduct

insula Roman apartments

Latin Language of the Romans

legion Roman army of around 5,000 citizen soldiers. The Roman Empire had between 25 and 30 of them

legionary Roman foot soldier, who was the basic unit of the Roman army

mosaic Picture made of many tiny pieces of colored tile, stone, or glass, pushed into cement

palla Shawl worn by Roman women

Roman women wore a stola (dress) and palla (shawl).

republic State ruled by elected officials instead of a king or emperor. The term is also used to describe the period, between 509–27 BCE, when Rome was ruled by elected officials

Roman Empire Lands and peoples ruled by the Romans. The term is also used to describe the period when Rome was ruled by emperors rather than by elected officials

Saturnalia Festival when masters served their slaves

Senate Roman governing council, made up of the most important Roman nobles. It gave advice to the emperor

slave Someone who is owned by another person as property

stola Dress worn by Roman women

stylus Pointed metal stick used to write on a tablet

summa rudis Referee in a gladiator fight

tablet Wooden frame filled with wax, used by children to practice writing

Roman men wore togas.

toga Wool gown worn by Roman male citizens. It was made of a single sheet wrapped around the body

triclinium Roman dining room with three couches for guests to lie down on

tunic Item of clothing worn by all Romans, made from two squares of material sewn together

wreath Crown of leaves, sometimes worn by Roman emperors

Index

Acknowledgments

The publisher would like to thank the following people for their assistance: Cecile Landau and Ruth O'Rourke for editorial assistance; Alexandra Beeden for proofreading; Helen Peters for compiling the index; Rob Nunn for picture research; Lol Johnson for photography; Sachin Singh for cutouts; and Daniel Long, Dan Crisp, and Ed Merritt for illustrations. The publishers would also like to thank the Roman and Barbarian warriors from Britannia (www.durolitum.co.uk) and the Gallic chieftan and auxilliary soldier from Portals to the Past (www.portalstothepast.co.uk).

The publisher would like to thank the following for their kind permission to reproduce their photographs:

(Key: a-above; b-below/bottom; c-center; f-far; l-left; r-right; t-top)

2 Rex Shutterstock: De Agostini / A. Dagli Orti (br). 3 Alamy Images: A. Astes (bl). Dorling Kindersley: Thackeray Medical Museum (bc); The University of Aberdeen (tr). 4-5 Alamy Images: Fine Art Images / Heritage Image Partnership Ltd. 11 Alamy Images: A. Astes (l). Dorling Kindersley: Ermine Street Guard (br). 12 Alamy Images: Lanmas (cra). Dorling Kindersley: Capitoline Museum, Rome (Musei Capitolini) (cl). 13 Alamy Images: Masterpics (tr). 14-15 Alamy Images: EmmePi Travel. 17 Dorling Kindersley: Ermine Street Guard (br). 18 Alamy Images: Michele Falzone (bl). Dorling Kindersley: Christi Graham and Nick Nicholls / The Trustees of the British Museum (ftr, ca). Rex Shutterstock: De Agostini / A. Dagli Orti (cl). 19 Dorling Kindersley: Odds Farm Park, High Wycombe, Bucks (clb); Thackeray Medical Museum (cr). Getty Images: Danita Delimont / Gallo Images (c). 20 Dorling Kindersley: Christi Graham and Nick Nicholls / The Trustees of the British Museum (tl, ca). 21 Corbis: Wolfgang Kaehler (b). 22 Photoshot: UPPA (br). 24 Alamy Images: Collection Dagli Orti / The Art Archive (tl). Bridgeman Images: Tarker (cr). Dorling Kindersley: Maidstone Museum and Bentliff Art Gallery (c). 25 Alamy Images: Lanmas (tr); World History Archive (tl). Dorling Kindersley: Tim Parmenter / The Trustees of the British Museum (cl); The Science Museum, London (cla). Getty Images: DEA Picture Library / De Agostini Picture Library (br); DEA / G. Dagli Orti / De Agostini Picture Library (fcl). 29 Alamy Images: Peter Phipp / Travelshots.com (cra). 32-33 Corbis: Alessandra Benedetti. 34 Dorling Kindersley: Thackeray Medical Museum (br, fbr). 35 Alamy

Images: Milleflore Images - Food and Tableware Misc (fcr); Bruce Miller (bl). Dorling Kindersley: Thackeray Medical Museum (tr, cra, cr). 36-37 Alamy Images: Lebrecht Music and Arts Photo Library. 37 Alamy Images: Gianni Dagli Orti / The Art Archive (cra). 38 Alamy Images: Art Nation (br). 39 Alamy Images: geogphotos (br). 40-41 Alamy Images: Lautaro. 42 Alamy Images: Granger, NYC (cb); Prisma Archivo (c); Stephen Dorey Creative (clb). Dorling Kindersley: Tim Draper / Rough Guides (cl). 42-43 Getty Images: DEA / S. Vannini / De Agostini (b). 43 Alamy Images: Reinhard Dirscherl (cl, cla); imageBROKER (cr). 46-47 Alamy Images: Aliaksei Verasovich. 52 Dorling Kindersley: Ermine Street Guard (tc). 54 Alamy Images: Walter Rawlings / robertharding (br). 54-55 Alamy Images: Vaclav Schindler. 55 Alamy Images: funkyfood London - Paul Williams (bl). Corbis: Gary Braasch (tr). Dorling Kindersley: Museo Archeologico Nazionale di Napoli (br). 56 Alamy Images: David A. Barnes (bl). Dorling Kindersley: Canterbury City Council, Museums and Galleries (cl). 57 Alamy Images: Sergey Borisov (clb). Corbis: Roger Wood (cla). 58 Dorling Kindersley: Thackeray Medical Museum (ca); Jerry Young (fcl). Dreamstime.com: Vladimir Korostyshevskiy / v0v (cr). Getty Images: De Agostini / L. Romano / De Agostini Picture Library (br). 59 Dorling Kindersley: The University of Aberdeen (tc). Endpapers: Front: Alamy Images: funkyfood London - Paul Williams (trajan); Massimiliano Pieraccini (constatine). Dorling Kindersley: The Trustees of the British Museum (coin); Tim Draper / Rough Guides (wall). Back: Alamy Images: Ian Bottle (hadrian's wall); Martin Garnham (rotunda of galerius); Amar and Isabelle Guillen - Guillen Photo LLC (kom el-dikka); Andrey Nekrasov (amphitheatre of thysdrus); OlegMit (pompeii); Stefano Politi Markovina (library of celsus); Premier (leptis magna); Michael Runkel / imageBROKER (ruins of djemila); Juergen

Schonnop (pont du gard); Vivienne Sharp / Imagestate Media Partners Limited - Impact Photos (temple of bacchus); Claude Thibault (tower of hercules). Corbis: Marco Cristofori (diocletian's palace).

All other images © Dorling Kindersley For further information see: www.dkimages.com

About the author

Peter Chrisp is an experienced author who has published more than 80 books on history for young readers. His special interest is in the ancient World, and he is the author of a number of Dorling Kindersley books, including *Ancient Rome Revealed*, *Ancient Greece Revealed*, *E. Explore: Ancient Rome*, *E. Explore: Ancient Greece*, and *Alexander the Great: Legend of a Warrior King*.

My Findout facts:

Roman buildings today

Hadrian's Wall
(frontier wall)
**England,
United Kingdom**
122–128CE

Pont du Gard
(aqueduct)
**Vers-Pont-du-Gard,
France**
1st century CE

Tower of Hercules
(lighthouse)
Coruña, Spain
1st century CE

Colosseum
(amphitheater)
Rome, Italy
70–80CE

Arch of Caracalla
(monument)
Volubus, Morocco
217CE

Ruins of Djemila
(ruined town)
Djemila, Algeria
2nd–6th centuries CE

Amphitheater of Thysdrus
El Djem, Tunisia
3rd century CE

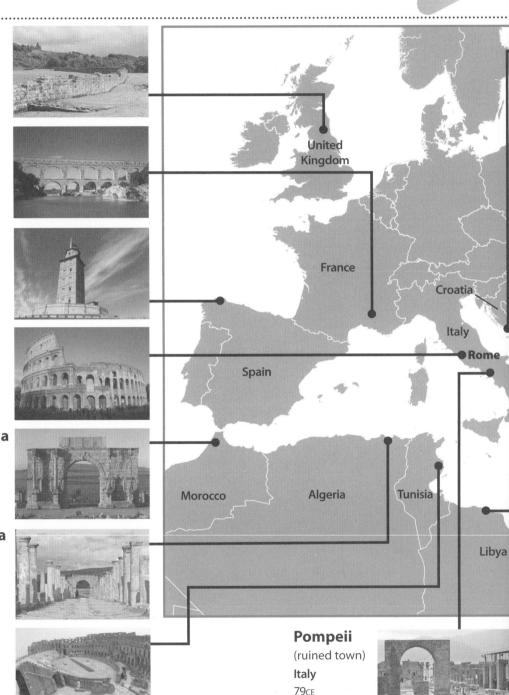

United Kingdom

France

Croatia

Italy

Rome

Spain

Morocco

Algeria

Tunisia

Libya

Pompeii
(ruined town)
Italy
79CE